Empowered Abundance: From Debt to Financial Success

5 Steps to Transform Your Relationship with Money

Dr. Thembi Aquil

Book Cover by Nasif Wright

ISBN

979-8-9918957-0-5 eBook

979-8-9918957-1-2 Paperback

Dedication

I dedicate this book to the strong women in my family who set powerful examples by managing their finances with confidence and independence. Their resilience and wisdom have been a source of inspiration, and I hope to carry their legacy forward through this work.

Acknowledgments

This book would not have been possible without the invaluable support of writer Lee Bernstein. Your guidance made all the difference.

I am also deeply grateful to those who took the time to read early drafts and provide thoughtful feedback—your insights were invaluable.

To my family and friends, thank you for your constant encouragement and belief in me throughout this journey.

Introduction

Transforming Your Money Mindset for a Life of Abundance

Welcome to *Empowered Abundance: From Debt to Financial Success - 5 Steps to Transform Your Relationship with Money*. You're about to make a liberating, positive change in your life, and guess what? You're about to get richer, too. Money worries shrink when you realize you have the tools and knowledge to handle whatever comes your way.

Changing how you think about money unlocks a world of possibilities. A positive attitude can help, but abundance takes more than optimism. Changing your money mindset is about sparking real, tangible changes in your life.

I'm Dr. Thembi Aquil, and I've been in your shoes. I've faced the overwhelming pressure of financial turmoil, and I know how hard it can be to discuss money problems with others, especially having to share your financial information.

But here's the thing—you don't need to be a financial expert to start turning things around, and you don't need a hefty bank account to fund finding peace and enjoyment. **Today marks a new beginning.**

Think of me as your financial buddy, here to guide you through the money maze, help you get a clear picture of where you stand, and give you a nudge to shift how you see and handle your cash.

Imagine hitting a giant reset button on your financial life. It's time to ditch unhelpful money beliefs and gear up for a fresh start.

Tweaking your relationship with money is like learning to play the piano. While learning overnight would be wonderful, you must track your progress, practice, seek guidance, and, most importantly, enjoy the tunes.

The magic happens when your new mindset and practical skills vibrate together. Your positive outlook keeps you motivated, while your money management turns those good vibes into success.

With over 25 years of experience working at Bank of America, I've gathered diverse experiences in financial well-being. Over half of my time at the bank was spent in the banking and lending departments, so I got to see the customers' financial struggles first-hand.

In addition to holding a Doctorate in Business Administration, my early career—helping with Junior Achievement and supporting families in transitional housing—also influenced my approach, along with these certifications:

- Workplace and Personal Wellness Foundations
- Building Empathy for Success
- Diversity, Equity, and Inclusion in the Workplace

I have also conducted Financial Wellness Workshops for Columbus Regional Health, Ultimate Medical Academy, Infinite Potential Learning Academy, and more.

As you can see, I love to help and support others during pivotal life moments.

Why? Because I've been through hell.

Picture this: I'm a college junior, discovering I'm about to be a mom. Fast-forward through a semester break to cuddle with my newborn, and there I was, back at it—juggling classes, a full-time job, and my tiny boss at home, my daughter.

Graduation came with a mix of triumph and exhaustion. At a moment when I longed for stability and a sprinkle of romance, an old friend unexpectedly reappeared, offering the companionship I craved.

After dating, getting married, and purchasing a home life threw me a curveball—I discovered I was pregnant while realizing my marriage was falling apart.

There I was, a solo mom with two kids, in an apartment as empty as my bank account—no furniture, no television, and nothing surrounding me except for my love for my children.

Making a home while caring for two kids? Hello, credit cards! At first, swiping a card was an easy fix, but debt soon became a burden. I remember how whenever the phone rang; it made me shiver. Each note hinted at a debt collector calling, ready with demands or bad news.

Amid mounting debts, my dwindling self-worth made me wonder if my financial challenges were eroding my role as a mother—the weight of the debt cast doubts on my ability to provide and care for my children, leaving me wondering if I was failing them in ways beyond my control. After all, if I couldn't take care of myself, how was I supposed to care for the two people I loved more than anything?

Desperation led me to knock on my dad's door, borrowing his old car after mine had to go because of bankruptcy. Talk about hitting rock bottom! But you know what? Hitting the lowest point means the only way is up. I landed a better job and hustled like never before, and bit by bit, our little home started to fill with more than just echoes.

Fast-forward a bit more, and there I was, keys to my car in hand, feeling like I'd just won the lottery. With all its bumps and bruises, that journey taught me some priceless lessons about money, resilience, and picking yourself up no matter how hard you fall.

So, here's the real talk: life's messy, unpredictable, and beautiful. My story isn't only about financial survival; it's about finding your feet, even when someone pulls the rug out from under you.

And guess what? If I can navigate those financial storms and emerge from the other side, so can you. Let's dive into this adventure together, shall we.

Contents

Chapter One

Understand Your Money Mindset

Are you drowning in debt?

Are you clueless about why you can't get ahead?

I'm Dr. Thembi Aquil, the Owner of Sensible Living, a Financial Wellness company specializing in uncovering money stories, financial trauma, and mastering one's money mindset.

I understand your stress about money running out before the month does. I've been there and climbed out (it took me multiple times to get it right), and now I use my experience and expertise to help people like you navigate the often-overwhelming world of personal finance.

Reading this book will give you access to my years of experience. Sensible Living offers personalized financial strategies to conquer money woes, enabling you to enjoy life with the ones you love. We have worked with countless individuals on personal and business finances and collaborated with companies to provide financial wellness workshops. I've gathered all the information here to help make your financial worries a thing of the past.

As a Certified Financial Educator and Housing Counselor, I have over 25 years of experience at Bank of America, working in Consumer Banking, Consumer Lending, and Procedure Management. During that time, I earned my master's degree and then a Doctorate in Business Administration (Saint Leo University). I am also a Freddie Mac CreditSmart Coach and FICO Credit Literacy Instructor. In 2010, I began teaching financial literacy to kids, teens, and adults.

The best part? What you'll learn here is fun and rewarding. Living a healthy financial lifestyle feels great, and getting there isn't nearly as difficult as you think. I've helped numerous people achieve financial peace of mind, replacing the stress of money with the confidence to reach their goals. In this book, I will help you, too.

Enjoy a How-To and Journaling Combo

I've created this book to be a complete guide. It provides detailed instructions on various financial subjects while allowing room for personal reflections and notes, essentially serving as a how-to manual and a journal.

Journaling with intent is important, as it can significantly impact your overall well-being. By dedicating time daily to reflect on your thoughts, experiences, and emotions, you will gain valuable insights, track your progress, and improve your mental clarity. You can use journaling for self-discovery, goal setting, or simply unwinding. As you will see, journaling is a powerful practice to enhance mindfulness and self-awareness. However, to experience a miracle, you must commit to making it a meaningful part of your daily routine. Get excited because you're about to witness the positive effects journaling will bring!

Financial Well-Being as a Way of Life

The first step towards financial wellness is understanding your money story. This means looking at your past experiences with money, whether positive or negative. A person's relationship with money often reflects their upbringing and history, and understanding these influences is crucial for developing healthy money habits and behaviors.

Have you noticed how people enthusiastically approach fitness and diets, only to be caught in a cycle of temporary changes that don't stick? It's a familiar scenario—hopping on the scale, setting goals to shed pounds, perhaps succeeding for a while, but ultimately reverting to old habits. And just like that, the weight creeps back on. This cycle can feel like a never-ending loop until the realization that **lasting change demands a fundamental shift in lifestyle**, not a quick fix.

Money is the same. Instead of sticking to a budget for a few months, the secret lies in changing how you think about money and how to enjoy interacting with every cent. And that doesn't mean depriving yourself. Sadly, most people view budgeting their money as restricting themselves from the pleasure of spending. Still, the truth is that budgeting, if done correctly, can lead to exhilarating rewards, including feeling better about yourself than you have in a long time. And yes, you can still buy and own things that add to your comfort and well-being.

I have good news for you. If you've tried to manage your finances and feel like you've failed, you have not. You are anything but a failure. Every setback is an opportunity to learn, adapt, and progress toward overcoming debt and managing finances effectively.

We will examine the roots of financial behaviors—your "Money Script." Your script takes shape early on; family, friends, and society all have an influence on your financial habits and attitudes.

For example, my money script includes always having a stocked pantry, a habit I've had since adulthood, based on experiences from my childhood. Quirks like these shape how you deal with money. Figuring out your money script is the first step in changing it up, so now it's time to explore your financial mindset:

Money Mindset Quiz

1. How do you feel when you receive a large bill unexpectedly?

A) Stressed and overwhelmed

B) Concerned but confident you can handle it

C) Excited about the challenge to solve it

2. What comes to mind first when you think of wealthy people?

A) They're lucky or dishonest

B) They're hardworking and smart

C) They're no different from anyone else; they just have more money

3. How do you approach saving money?

A) It's tough; I don't have enough to save

B) I save regularly, but it feels like a chore

C) Saving is empowering; it's building my future

4. What's your reaction to the idea of budgeting?

A) It's restrictive and stressful

B) It's necessary but not enjoyable

C) It's a useful tool to achieve financial freedom

5. How do you feel about setting long-term financial goals?

A) It feels pointless; things change too much to plan that far ahead

B) I set goals, but sticking to them is a challenge

C) I find it motivating; it helps me stay focused on my future

6. When discussing money with friends or family, you tend to:

A) Avoid the topic altogether

B) Talk about it openly but with caution

C) Share openly and offer/receive advice

7. How do you feel about investing your money?

A) It seems risky and out of reach

B) I'm interested but unsure where to start

C) Investing is a strategic way to grow my wealth

If you chose mostly A's, you might have a scarcity mindset, viewing money as a constant source of stress. More B's suggests a balanced but cautious approach to money. The C's mostly show a growth mindset, viewing money as a tool for empowerment and opportunities.

You probably answered mostly A's, or you wouldn't be reading this book. But you still need a reset if you answered mostly B's.

Fear of Success? *Seriously?*

At the start of this chapter, I drew a parallel between diet and money, and I have an anecdote to share on this comparison.

I have a friend, a remarkable woman, who once led weight-loss meetings and was an engaging public speaker. One of her most compelling presentations resonated deeply with many: the fear of failure versus success. While most of us readily admit to fearing failure, she introduced the fear of success as a less considered but equally potent fear.

In her talks, she would pose a thought-provoking question about how people perceived those who were thin, fit, or conventionally attractive. "When you were growing up, or even now," she'd ask, "how do you view beautiful, thin people? Do you admire them, or do you harbor resentment or envy?" She encouraged her audience to reflect on their family's attitudes as well. Were thin people lauded in their households, or were they the subject of disdain?

This inquiry often sparked a collective moment of realization among her audience. Many found their feelings about thin people were more complex than they thought. Some felt a hidden resentment or envy—emotions they hadn't consciously linked to their fear of success. This aha moment was revealing; it uncovered a subconscious, erroneous belief that becoming more attractive could result in others disliking them.

So, let's touch on a topic seldom explored—fear of success. How did you view wealthy people as a child? Were they the villains in your story, or were they inspirations?

I am not a psychologist or psychiatrist, and neither is my friend, but her insights into the fear of success in terms of physical appearance opened a new avenue of thought for me. It made me ponder: could the same principle apply to financial lives? Just as some might subconsciously fear becoming more attractive due to potential negative social repercussions, might they also, on some level, fear achieving financial success?

Consider this: on the surface, aspiring to wealth seems universally desirable. But looking deeper, you might uncover apprehension about the social implications of becoming wealthy.

Reflect on how your family or social circle perceived wealthy individuals. Did they admire rich people, or was there a resentment or suspicion? Were affluent people depicted as greedy or selfish in your upbringing? Here's another one: Have you ever witnessed someone become successful only to "fail?" For example, someone who gets terminally ill a month after *finally* retiring, a once happily married couple who divorces after winning the lottery, or a business executive who suffers from anxiety following a substantial raise. The truth is that the above examples had underlying issues before wealth happened. Money may have magnified the problems, but money didn't cause them. Situations like these can make you think that getting rich could make life harder. But that's not true! And there are tons more examples of people becoming more miserable from poverty than prosperity.

Good things bring happiness. Facing and understanding hidden fears helps you reach your money goals with a clear mind. Getting out of debt (or getting rich) won't make life tougher. Think about all the people who are happier when they have more than when they have less.

Simply put, prosperity is prosperity—nothing more, nothing less. Receiving a windfall of cash does not guarantee instant unhappiness or happiness. While financial wealth can open doors and provide opportunities, true prosperity encompasses well-being, contentment, and fulfillment beyond material possessions—it's about achieving a state of abundance in all aspects of life, including relationships, health, personal growth, and happiness.

So, while money can make life more comfortable, true prosperity is a holistic blend of wealth, purpose, and joy. This book aims to help you with everything so you can enjoy it fully when you achieve financial health. Confronting your hidden fears is the first step to reaching your financial goals with a clearer mindset.

REFLECTION QUESTIONS

I've provided ample writing space and engaging exercises in this book. It's time to get ready to win!

First, I have a few questions:

1- Do you dislike journaling?

2- Or do you enjoy journaling but put it off?

3- Would you seize the opportunity if someone promised you a million dollars in exchange for doing every exercise in this book without procrastinating? You'd jump at the chance, right?

If you're like many, recording or writing your thoughts may seem like too much work, but if you take the time to do every exercise in every chapter, your brain will strengthen, grow, and expand in ways you never thought possible. While the promise of a million dollars is hypothetical, it may be true. You'll never know until you try. So, do yourself a favor: Be a kid again. Revisit the world of make-believe. Pretend. Convince yourself that a million-dollar reward awaits by diligently completing the exercises in this book and truly embracing each piece of advice.

Tip: While I recommend writing or typing your journal entries, if writing is not your preference, you can record your answers using free "voice writing" in Word or Google Docs.

We'll start by looking at the feelings you have about money:

Did you receive an allowance as a child?

How did you feel about the amount you received compared to your peers?

Were there ever times you felt embarrassed by your home, car, or clothes when comparing them to your friends' possessions?

Looking back, do you think you had more or less financial stability than your friends? How did that make you feel at the time?

Did you feel that your financial situation as a child limited your opportunities or experiences compared to others?

Were you taught how to manage money effectively as a child, such as saving or budgeting? If so, who taught you, and how?

Did you ever need to hide your financial situation from friends or teachers? Why?

How did your family's financial situation influence the activities or hobbies you could participate in during your childhood?

Reflecting on your childhood, how do you think your early financial experiences have shaped your current attitudes toward money and success?

How did you do? Did you have any eye-opening moments?

As you continue with the exercises in this book, feel free to add to your journal entries or revisit them for reflection.

Congratulations! You've taken your first step toward transforming your relationship with money.

Understanding your financial blueprint sets the stage for meaningful change. You are now beginning to shift your mindset and see money as an ally in building success, not a source of endless struggle. By fostering a positive, empowered approach to money, you break free from the cycle of financial stress.

Are you ready to take it to the next level? That's what the next chapter will do.

CHAPTER TWO

Transforming Your Relationship with Money

Welcome to falling in love with success. Imagine turning feelings of envy into bursts of inspiration, limitations into new opportunities, and fear into empowerment. Sounds amazing, right? That's precisely what you will do—make your money work for you!

First, let's challenge any negative beliefs you might have about money. If you've ever thought, "I'll never be wealthy," change that to, "I can build wealth by making smart choices." Every time you think negatively about money, stop and replace that thought with something positive and encouraging. As another example, instead of saying, "I can't afford this," say, "I'm choosing to save for something more important."

Next, think of achieving prosperity as your new hobby. Start with this book but keep going. Many great workshops, podcasts, and online courses about personal finance exist. Make learning something new an exciting part of your week. Listen to a podcast during your commute or read a chapter of a financial book before bed.

I recommend *NerdWallet's Smart Money Podcast* and for a book, *The Psychology of Money* by Morgan Housel. As you learn more, you'll find you enjoy it! If you require assistance understanding or incorporating these exercises, I invite you to collaborate with me individually. Go to my website for more information: https://www.sensiblelivingcoach.com.

Set Clear Goals

What does financial success look like to you? It's different for everyone. It could be living without debt, owning a home, or having a solid emergency fund. Your goals should match your personality and what makes you excited about life. When your goals align with your dreams and values, they become powerful motivators, driving you to take action and achieve prosperity—dream-driven goals.

Dream-focused goals are powerful. A Journal of Applied Psychology study explored how internal motivation drives success. Strong desire stems from aligning personal goals with your values. For example, imagine you value financial security because it gives you peace of mind and the ability to care for your family. You set a personal goal to build an emergency fund that covers six months of living expenses. Because this goal aligns with your core values of security and providing for your loved ones, you *strongly* desire to prioritize saving money, and you find yourself motivated to cut unnecessary expenses, create a budget, and put aside a portion of your income each month. The same is true when saving for a vacation or anything that is deeply significant for you.

If you align your goals with your feelings, that is, a strong inner drive, you are more likely to work through obstacles and achieve your goals. Setting goals aligned with values and dreams enhances motivation and satisfaction because your goals excite you. Feeling good about goals and looking forward to completing them helps you stay focused and clear, making it easier to bounce back from challenges.

A research study from the Academy of Management Journal examined how workers feel about their values matching their company's values. The study found that when values align, employees are more engaged in their work, happier, and do better.

Employees whose goals aligned with their organization's values were more motivated and productive. This alignment helped them feel a stronger connection to their work, leading to better outcomes for both the individuals and the organization.

Another study published in *Psychological Science* demonstrated that people who set goals that were meaningful and aligned with their values were more likely to stick with their goals and experience greater well-being.

The empirical evidence is clear: aligning your goals with your dreams and values significantly boosts your motivation and likelihood of success. By setting goals that reflect what truly matters to you, you create a powerful internal drive that helps you overcome obstacles and stay committed to your path. Whether in personal endeavors or organizational settings, aligning goals and values is a proven strategy for achieving prosperity and fulfillment.

It's time to discover your dream-driven goals with the Imagination Exercises on the next page.

Dream-Driven Goal Exercises

This exercise has two parts. The first will clarify your wants, and the second will help you define them.

Dream-Driven Goal Exercises, Part One

Your Hopes:

- Why did you pick up this book?

- What do you hope to change or gain?

Identify Your Core Values:

- What are the top three values that guide your decisions and actions in life?

- How do these values influence your financial decisions?

Visualize Your Ideal Lifestyle:

- Describe your ideal day from morning to night. What activities are you doing? Who are you with?

- How does your financial situation support this ideal lifestyle?

Define Your Aspirations:

- What are your top three long-term goals (e.g., homeownership, traveling the world, starting a business)?

- Why are these goals important to you?

Connect Goals to Excitement:

- What aspects of financial wellness excite you the most?

- How do you feel when you think about financial wellness?

Short-Term and Long-Term Goals:

- What short-term financial goals do you want to achieve next year?

- What are three long-term financial goals you want to achieve in the next five to ten years?

Aligning Goals with Values:

- How do your financial goals reflect your core values?

- In what ways will achieving these goals enhance your life and align with your values?

Motivational Triggers:

- What motivates you to achieve your financial goals? (e.g., security, freedom, family, adventure)

- How can you incorporate these motivators into your daily routine to stay focused on your goals?

Overcoming Obstacles:

**- What potential obstacles might you face in achieving your
financial goals?**

**- How can you prepare or adjust your plans to overcome these
obstacles?**

Celebrate Successes:

- How will you celebrate when you achieve your short-term financial goals?

- What will you do to celebrate when you reach your long-term financial milestones?

Reflect and Adjust:

- How often will you review and adjust your financial goals to ensure they remain aligned with your values and aspirations?

- What steps will you take if you realize your goals no longer excite or motivate you?

Daily Habits and Actions:

- What daily habits can you develop to bring you closer to your financial goals?

- How can you make these habits enjoyable and fulfilling?

Support System:

- Who can you rely on for support and encouragement as you work towards your financial goals?

- How can you involve them in your journey to stay accountable and motivated?

And now: What are your ultimate financial goals?

List as many as you can without editing yourself. Start by sticking to the basics (get out of debt, take a vacation, etc.), then include your wildest dreams.

Goals:

Dream-Driven Goal Exercises, Part Two

This set of exercises is similar to Part One, but it will help you better define your dreams. First, answer each question. Then, break down your dreams into smaller, actionable steps.

For example, if your goal is to save for a down payment on a house, start by figuring out how much you need to save each month. Open a separate savings account just for this purpose and set up an automatic transfer to that account every month. Watching your savings grow will keep you motivated.

Another example: List all your debts from smallest to largest if you want to pay off debt. Start by paying extra on the smallest debt while making minimum payments on the others. Once you've paid off the smallest debt, move on to the next one. This method, known as the "snowball method," can give you quick wins and keep you motivated.

Close your eyes and imagine your life in five years while considering everything you've written. Write down everything you see and feel. This vision will help you set specific, clear goals.

1a- What does financial success mean to you? List everything you'd love to have in your life. Is it travel, education, or having the ability to take on a special job or project? Whatever your goals, they should excite you and make you feel fabulous.

1b- What small, actionable steps can you take to realize financial success?

2a- What do you see yourself doing five years from now? Use your imagination and have fun with this. When considering your response, aim to feel thrilled. Keep thinking until you find an answer where you smile with delight.

2b- What small, actionable steps can you take to realize your five-year dream?

3a- Where are you living? Write this answer in great detail. Include the location—city, state, and even the Zip Code if you have it. What does your home look like? How is it decorated? What do you most love about it?

3b- What small, actionable steps can you take to realize the home of your dreams?

4- What projects are you working on five years from now? Your projects can be anything from traveling the world to writing a best-selling novel; you can list as many as you like. Why are these projects important to you? How will they bring you joy?

5a- In reflecting on your answers, How does it feel to be financially secure? Again, write your answer in detail. Instead of writing "I feel great," write *why* you feel great. What are you most grateful for? In what ways has your life become more comfortable and enjoyable?

Review your responses carefully. After addressing the questions, you'll have the beginning of a roadmap to steer your financial path.

Regardless of your wants, **your financial goals should be clear and deeply connected to what <u>excites</u> and <u>motivates</u> you—this is important.** If your goals align with your values, aspirations, and the lifestyle you envision for yourself, they become powerful motivators, driving you to take consistent actions toward achieving prosperity.

A question: Have you been jotting down your answers or just breezing through? If you choose the latter, hold up! No procrastination is allowed here. Trust me, jot down your goals before you continue with this book. You can always tweak your answers later if needed.

Ready to turn your dreams into a solid plan? Let's dive in!

CHAPTER THREE

An Attitude of Gratitude

I want to share a story about Oprah Winfrey, one of the world's most famous and influential women. Oprah worked hard to achieve success. She grew up in poverty, overcame many challenges, and faced personal and professional setbacks. Throughout it all, Oprah held onto a practice she believed played a huge role in her success and happiness: gratitude.

Oprah often talks about how gratitude has made a big difference in her life. In the 1990s, she started jotting down five things she was thankful for daily. This simple habit helped her see the good things in her life, even during tough times.

In her book *What I Know For Sure*, Oprah shares how this practice changed her life. She wrote, "I know for sure that if you focus on what you have, you will always end up having more. If you focus on what you don't have, you will never, ever have enough" (Winfrey, 2014). By being grateful, Oprah learned to see abundance rather than scarcity.

When things got hard, Oprah found strength and resilience through gratitude. Take the example of her film *Beloved* not doing well at the box office. Instead of dwelling on the disappointment, she focused on the positive side—the lessons learned and the joy she got from the project.

This positive outlook helped Oprah keep moving forward with grace and determination. She went on to expand her media empire, start the Oprah Winfrey Network (OWN), and use her influence to inspire many. Oprah always stresses that gratitude plays a big role in her success and well-being.

In her book, What I Know for Sure (Flatiron Books), Oprah Winfrey shows us that being thankful can change how you see life and deal with challenges. So, take time daily to appreciate the good things, no matter how small. Oprah believes, "The more you praise and celebrate your life, the more there is in life to celebrate." (Winfrey, 2014).

Practicing gratitude is a powerful tool for transforming your financial mindset from scarcity to abundance. It's easy to get caught up in what you lack or want, especially regarding finances. However, taking a moment to appreciate what you already have will shift your relationship with money.

Reflecting on the time when my children and I lived in an empty apartment, I remind myself that I could have dwelled on what we lacked. However, doing so would have only intensified feelings of anger and frustration. Instead, I chose to focus on the joy we shared as a family, finding reasons to be grateful for the moments of peace and happiness we experienced together.

Acknowledging the positive aspects of your current financial situation, whether small or seemingly insignificant, nurtures a sense of contentment and abundance—this could be as simple as being grateful for your last meal or having the smallest savings. When you focus on what you have rather than what you're missing, you see your financial situation differently.

Gratitude also can reduce stress and anxiety, emotions often associated with financial concerns. By appreciating what you already have, you're less likely to feel overwhelmed by what you don't. This shift in mindset can open up a clearer path to setting and achieving your financial goals because you're approaching them from a place of positivity and abundance, not lack or fear.

Moreover, practicing gratitude can enhance your decision-making process. When you're grateful and content with what you have, you're less likely to make impulsive financial decisions spurred by feelings of scarcity or the desire to fill a perceived void. Instead, you make choices that align more closely with your long-term goals and values (and you'll even enjoy doing it).

Start by keeping a gratitude journal, focusing specifically on financial aspects. Each day, jot down three financial things you're grateful for. Over time, you'll notice a shift in how you view your finances and your overall approach to money management. By cultivating gratitude, you're enriching happiness and fulfillment.

Develop a Budget That Reflects Your Values: Instead of seeing a budget as a constraint, view it as a map guiding you to your financial goals. Allocate funds for necessities and things that bring joy and fulfillment (more to come later in this book).

Build a Support System: Like a gym buddy, having a financial accountability partner can keep you motivated and on track. We'll discuss this more, but for now, you've already taken this step. I'm your financial buddy, and I have your back.

As you work through this book, you may find areas where you need extra guidance or support. I'm here to help you navigate your financial success so you're getting the most out of what you've learned. If you want personalized advice or more accountability, I also offer coaching packages to guide you through the book's content step-by-step.

Now, it's time to be grateful. Every day, for one month, fill each of the following pages with everything you're thankful for—this will help you stop dreaming and make a plan.

A Month of Gratitude

What brings you gratitude today? Daily, jot down numerous blessings on each page. Repeating some items is fine but strive for fresh responses. The more you write, the more ideas will come to you.

Day 1

Day 2

Day 3

Day 4

Day 5

Day 6

Day 7

Day 8

Day 9

Day 10

Day 11

Day 12

Day 13

Day 14

Day 15

Day 16

Day 17

Day 18

Day 19

Day 20

Day 21

Day 22

Day 23

Day 24

Day 25

Day 26

Day 27

Day 28

Day 29

Day 30

Day 31

You did it! Now, it's time to stop dreaming and make a plan.

The next chapter is about combining your dreams, passions, and goals into a plan that feels right for you.

CHAPTER FOUR

Mindful Spending

Debt, Anyone?

Back in college, signing up for credit cards for freebies led me into debt. When we're young, it's easy to feel invincible and delay saving or make questionable financial choices. It's also easy to say, "I can handle a credit card!" By offering enticing gifts, credit card companies often target college students as potential new cardholders. These promotions can include anything from T-shirts and water bottles to more substantial items like tech gadgets or gift cards.

The strategy plays on the excitement and independence of college life, appealing to students eager to make their own financial decisions. However, while appealing, these gifts can mask the more significant commitments and risks associated with owning and using a credit card, such as interest rates and the potential for accumulating debt.

Knowing what I know now, I never would have opened credit cards in college, and I would have started saving for retirement immediately after graduating.

But here's the thing: No matter our age, many of us think we can handle credit cards without debt. But the reality is tougher. Credit cards can make you feel secure, tempting you to spend money you don't have. This way of thinking, high-interest rates, and potential fees can quickly turn small purchases into big debt. Keeping an eye on your spending and paying off balances each month is key to steering clear of the debt spiral credit cards can drag you into.

I had to chuckle as I read what I had just written. Telling someone who wants to be financially secure to "spend less, save more, and pay bills on time" has the same appeal as telling someone who wants to lose weight to "eat less and exercise more." Yeah, it's great in theory and works, but try to do it in real life!

The good news is that financial security is easier than it seems. If you're in debt now, or if you're not in debt but still have trouble getting by, there are ways to turn things around, and you don't have to do it alone. I am here to help you, as are numerous experts.

I once worked with a client who would go shopping on payday and struggle to get by until the next paycheck. I mean nothing left!!! Eventually, they got tired of living like that and reached out for help. Through months of coaching, accountability, and consistent reminders, they developed healthier spending habits. Today, they're more mindful of their money and have come to appreciate the importance of saving. This doesn't mean they no longer go shopping, but now it is with a budget based on how much they have saved.

Let's begin with an exercise:

Mindful Spending Journal Exercise

This exercise will help you gain clarity on your spending habits and align them with your financial goals. Take some time to reflect on each question and write your thoughts in your journal. The more honest and detailed you are, the more valuable this exercise will be.

Think back to your last few non-essential purchases. What motivated you to spend money on these items or experiences?

Were these purchases planned or impulsive? How did you feel before, during, and after making them?

Did these purchases bring you lasting satisfaction or only temporary pleasure? Why do you think that is?

Look at your spending over the past month. Do you notice any patterns? Are there certain times of the day, situations, or emotions that lead you to spend more?

What are your biggest spending triggers? Is it boredom, stress, social pressure, or something else? How can you manage these triggers more effectively?

Review your financial goals. Do your recent spending habits support or hinder these goals?

Which expenses align with your values and long-term aspirations? Which ones don't? How can you adjust your spending to better reflect your goals?

What are three things you could cut back on or eliminate entirely? How will redirecting this money help you achieve your financial goals faster?

Set a spending limit for the week or month. How will you stick to this limit? What strategies can you use to avoid unnecessary spending?

Create a "want vs. need" list. The next time you're tempted to buy something, ask yourself: Is this a want or a need? How will this purchase impact my financial goals?

Commit to a cooling-off period. For non-essential purchases, give yourself 24 hours (or more) before making a decision. How often do you think this will help you avoid impulse buys? How did you feel when you tried this step?

At the end of each week, review your spending. How well did you stick to your plan? What did you learn about your habits?

Celebrate small victories. Did you resist a temptation or find a new way to save money? Acknowledge these successes, no matter how small.

Set new goals based on your reflections. What changes will you make next week to continue improving your spending habits?

How do you currently feel about your debt? Does it cause you stress or anxiety? What steps can you take to begin reducing your debt and feeling more in control?

What actions will you take this month to manage or reduce your debt? Will you negotiate with creditors, cut non-essential spending, or increase your income? How will these actions bring you closer to financial freedom?

Congratulations on completing this exercise. By regularly journaling your thoughts and progress, you're developing a deeper understanding of your spending habits and how they align with your financial goals. You're now in a better place to make more mindful decisions toward a more secure and prosperous future.

Debt Dilemma Resources

Here are some tools to help you with your financial remake:

Online Tools and Apps: Various apps and websites offer budgeting, debt tracking, and financial planning tools. Examples include Simply Budget, YNAB (You Need a Budget), and PocketGuard, which help you monitor expenses and manage debt repayment plans effectively.

Books and Educational Materials: Educating yourself about personal finance is a must. Of course, if you're reading this book, you've already begun, but I recommend reading as many as you comfortably can. Books like Dave Ramsey's *The Total Money Makeover* or Vicki Robin's *Your Money or Your Life* give insights into managing money and getting out of debt.

Community Resources: Check with local community centers or libraries for workshops, classes, or personal finance and debt management seminars. Operation Hope offers services for individuals and small business owners.

Online Forums and Support Groups: Websites like Reddit's r/personalfinance or Instagram's Debt Free Community can offer moral support and advice from others who have faced or are facing similar challenges.

Government Resources: Websites like USA.gov and the Consumer Financial Protection Bureau provide resources and tips on handling debt and understanding your rights as a consumer.

Bankruptcy Attorneys: Consulting with a bankruptcy attorney can help you understand your legal options, including Chapter 7 and Chapter 13 bankruptcy, as a last resort. Bankruptcy can provide a fresh start but has significant consequences, including a substantial impact on your credit history.

Financial Coach: A good financial coach gets to know you, has your back, and often takes considerable time to make sure you achieve your financial goals.

It's important to thoroughly research and consider the reputation and fees of any service before committing. Avoid organizations that promise quick fixes or charge high upfront fees. Reputable organizations will offer a free initial consultation on long-term solutions tailored to your needs.

Handling Debt

Whether you're working with a debt support team or handling matters yourself, these are steps to keep in mind:

Negotiate with Creditors: Contact your creditors to negotiate lower interest rates or modified repayment plans. Many creditors are willing to work with consumers to adjust repayment terms.

Cut Non-Essential Spending: Review your budget for any non-essential expenses you can reduce or eliminate. Redirecting this money towards your debt can accelerate your payoff.

Increase Your Income: Look for ways to increase your income, such as taking on a part-time job, selling unused items, or doing freelance work.

Set Clear Goals and Track Your Progress: Stay motivated by setting clear, achievable goals for your debt reduction. Regularly track your progress to see how much you've paid off and how much closer you are to debt-free.

Stay Persistent and Patient: Debt repayment is a marathon, not a sprint. Stay persistent with your efforts and patient with the process. Celebrate small victories along the way to keep yourself motivated.

Saving Matters

Your Income WANTS to Reward You

Meet Emily.

Fresh out of college, Emily landed her first job at a local library, earning a modest salary. Unlike many of her peers, Emily had a keen interest in personal finance, a passion ignited by a seminar on the magic of compound interest.

Intrigued by the concept, Emily decided to test the compound interest theory. She opened a retirement investment account, committing to set aside $200 each month. The account had ups and downs but averaged a conservative annual return of 6% compounded monthly.

Time passed, and life brought its fair share of challenges and changes. Emily experienced job changes, a marriage, and the birth of her children. But her $200 monthly contribution remained constant throughout. It helped that Emily "paid herself first"—investing before spending—and had the $200 automatically deposited into her account each month, so she never missed a deposit.

On her 52nd birthday, Emily sat down to review her finances, and to her amazement, her initial modest contributions had grown significantly. Her account now boasted a substantial sum of $170,000. Emily marveled at how her small but consistent savings had compounded over the years, growing into a sizable nest egg.

Excited by this financial milestone, she shared her story with friends and family, hoping to inspire them with the tangible results of compound interest. Emily explained how investing early helped, allowing her contributions more time to grow. She highlighted how her disciplined approach and the continuous effect of compounding had steadily built her wealth even during years when the market dipped.

But it gets better. The $170,000 only represents what Emily made from $200 a month. Over the years, she opened additional accounts, including taking advantage of work benefits (see below), and she increased her contributions as her earnings increased. By the time she retired, her diligent savings strategy, powered by the quiet force of compound interest, had transformed her initial modest contributions into a retirement fund that exceeded $500,000.

Emily spent her retirement years traveling, indulging in hobbies, and enjoying time with her grandchildren, all funded by the foresight and financial discipline she had practiced since her early twenties. Her story became a favorite lesson she loved to pass on to her grandchildren, teaching them the value of saving early and letting compound interest do the heavy lifting. Emily's practical approach to saving and the conservative yet steady growth of her investments ensured that her golden years were as golden as they could be, proving that sometimes, the most ordinary beginnings can lead to extraordinary endings.

Note: **Yes, Emily started young, but if you're older, stay positive.** While you may have a different time horizon than Emily, you can still employ effective strategies. I know many people who didn't learn how to save until middle age, and they still learned how to live comfortably.

-First, assess your current financial situation and define achievable goals. Consider increasing the amount you save each month; even small increases can make a significant difference over time.

-Look into catch-up contributions, which allow those over 50 to contribute additional funds to retirement accounts. Prioritize high-interest debts to free up more money for savings.

-Consult with a financial advisor to tailor a plan that maximizes your resources and addresses your financial needs. Every step you take now will lead to a more secure financial future.

Unlock Additional Income with Workplace Benefits

When managing your finances, make the most of all your work perks, especially those related to benefits. Get to know the savings plans your employer provides like 401(k)s, 403(b)s (for non-profit folks), HSAs, and FSAs. Each plan has its perks, from tax advantages to employer contributions and tax-free withdrawals for medical costs.

Take note of employer match programs for retirement plans like the 401(k). If your employer matches contributions, contribute at least enough to capture the full benefit. Think of this as free money, which immediately boosts your investment returns.

Contributions to these plans typically offer tax advantages, reducing your taxable income and lowering your annual tax bill—this can provide immediate relief, freeing additional funds for other expenses or investments.

It's also crucial to align your investments with your long-term financial goals. Whether planning to buy a home or preparing for an early retirement, your goals will dictate how best to utilize your savings options. Speak to a financial professional and periodically review your goals so your investment strategy stays on track.

Discuss the importance of diversification and risk management, particularly as you approach retirement. Adjusting your investment strategy to include more conservative options can protect your savings from market volatility.

Stop Sighing. You're Not Dying.

If all of this seems overwhelming, you're not alone. You're also not dying, so stop sighing and stop thinking; this *is all too much and meant for someone else. I can hardly breathe.* Well, if this book isn't meant for you, who is it meant for? The truth is, it's crafted just for you—yes, you! You're the star of a financial success story waiting to happen. A question:

Have you ever seen the movie *What About Bob*?

What About Bob is a 1991 comedy film starring Bill Murray as Bob Wiley, a highly dependent and phobic patient who seeks help from a psychiatrist, Dr. Leo Marvin, played by Richard Dreyfuss. Dr. Marvin introduces Bob to his self-help book, *Baby Steps*, which outlines small, manageable goals to overcome overwhelming anxieties gradually.

The concept of "baby steps" becomes a central theme throughout the film, as Bob takes the advice literally, leading to many laughs. **But the point I'm making is serious.**

Everything seems overwhelming to you right now because you're looking at the big picture—it's like standing at the base of The Empire State Building, wondering how you'll get to the top.

Imagine this: each financial goal you set is like taking an elevator up one floor at a time. All you need to do is push the button and ride up slowly, floor by floor.

You'll feel more confident and at ease with each level you reach. **Whether you realize it or not, you already have everything you need inside you.** Each step brings you closer to your goals and helps you feel more relaxed and in control. Keep pushing those buttons, and you'll soon realize your ability to reach the top.

Now, let's push a few more:

Spending Habits

Play a game for a month by turning your spending into a financial scavenger hunt. Challenge yourself to identify where every dollar goes. A fun and interactive app called YNAB (You Need A Budget) can transform tracking your spending into a game-like experience. YNAB makes managing your money fun by encouraging you to "give every dollar a job." The app focuses on budgeting but does it in a way that makes it feel like you're strategically planning each move of your financial life, much like a game.

Other apps that add a bit of fun to the mix are Simply Budget (completely free) and PocketGuard (basic subscription free). They are visually appealing and user-friendly, offering features that help you track your spending, set up budgets, and see where your money goes through colorful charts and graphs. They also send alerts and insights to help keep you on your toes and make the process more interactive.

If an app isn't your style, go classic with a colorful notebook or detailed spreadsheet. At month-end, play detective with your data. Categorize your expenses into "essentials" and "non-essentials." Identify patterns and surprises—maybe you're a pizza connoisseur or outdoor gear enthusiast. Knowing how you spend your money is the initial phase.

As life evolves, your goals may shift. Continuously evaluate and adapt your focus. I conduct a thorough budget analysis for new clients, documenting every cost, even for streaming services. Ask yourself: does this expense align with my financial goals? If not, cut back. Prioritize spending on what's important to you, whether that's travel, an emergency fund, or becoming debt-free.

Master your finances: Yes, You Can, and YES, YOU WILL

This chapter carries a straightforward message: Mastering your finances might initially seem daunting, but it's achievable with a clear strategy and consistent effort. Managing your money is about establishing small, sustainable habits that build over time.

Applying the principles discussed in this chapter—tracking your spending, understanding where your money goes, and aligning your expenses with your financial goals—you'll likely become more comfortable and confident with your financial decisions.

Every step you take towards understanding and controlling your finances brings you closer to a more secure financial future. Stick with the process, adjust as necessary, and keep your end goals in sight. You're capable of succeeding, and the elevator door is open.

Next: Do you think it's possible to enjoy budgeting? I mean REALLY enjoy it. Whether yes or no, the next chapter will enlighten you and help bring joy.

CHAPTER FIVE

Make Budgeting Fun

Do you enjoy budgeting? If you're reading this book, the answer is probably "No" or "I try to keep a budget, but I hate it!"Many people feel they need to improve their budgeting skills. It's normal, and having a supportive environment helps. Start by taking a look at your life. Was budgeting an important part? If not, begin by acknowledging, "I never learned budgeting," or "Saving wasn't important in my life," and tell yourself it's okay. Loving yourself is the first step to financial success.

Try reframing budgeting not as a chore but as a valuable tool for achieving your personal and financial goals.

Several famous people have changed their minds about money and budgeting. One of my favorite examples is the basketball legend Shaquille O'Neal. Early on, he was like many young athletes—he had money but lacked money management skills. On season 6, episode 607 of *Oprah's Master Class*, Shaq spoke about being caught up in his newfound wealth. He even spent a million dollars in a day!

After his banker helped him recognize his unsustainable spending habits, Shaq shifted his mindset and educated himself on budgeting, investing, and saving, changing his wealth approach—much like you are doing now.

Another example is Robert Kiyosaki, author of "Rich Dad Poor Dad." Kiyosaki's philosophy revolves around using money and budgeting as tools to build wealth. His approach sees money management as a necessity and a path to financial freedom.

And Then, There's Wonderful, Lovable You

Let's pretend this is your story:

Once upon a time, you lived a life filled with spontaneous adventures and impulse buys. While exciting, this lifestyle left your bank account dry.

Although friends and family hinted at the wisdom of budgeting, the thought of spreadsheets and expense tracking made you cringe. But one evening, while stressing over bills, you had an eye-opening experience. It was almost like an angel whispered in your ear, "You're looking the wrong way! You're missing out on all the fun! When you learn to look at what you spend, you'll learn that **controlling your destiny is your superpower.**"*My superpower?* You thought. *Is it possible that budgeting holds amazement? Maybe it's not about giving up things but rather about seeking happiness and freedom. Could each number I record bring me joy?*

A bubble of excitement swelled as you realized that understanding where your money goes could be—dare you think it—fun.

And then, a miracle happened. There's something special about realizing that understanding money feels better than splurging.

That's right. **Understanding where your money flows is more satisfying than spending it.**When you consider whether a purchase will improve your life, you engage in "reflective consumption." This practice taps into higher-level cognitive processes, such as self-reflection and long-term planning, which are important for making choices that align with your goals.

This mindful approach to spending activates your brain's prefrontal cortex, the area responsible for executive functions like focus, impulse control, and foreseeing future consequences. By considering the long-term impact of your purchases, you're exercising mental muscles that build stronger willpower and self-discipline.

The concept of "reflective consumption" aligns with various psychological theories and findings that emphasize the importance of self-reflection and deliberate decision-making in achieving personal goals. Psychologist Daniel Kahneman's work supports this idea, particularly in his book *Thinking, Fast and Slow*. Kahneman distinguishes between two modes of thought: "System 1", which is fast, instinctive, and emotional, and "System 2", which is slower, deliberate, and logical. Reflective consumption taps into "System 2," engaging higher-level cognitive processes necessary for thoughtful decision-making.

Moreover, behavioral economics focuses on the perks of thoughtful decision-making in financial actions, like the work of Nobel Laureate Richard H. Thaler. Thaler's ideas on "mental accounting" back the notion that being mindful of spending can improve financial and personal results.

Trust me, it's amazing how powerful a mindful approach to spending can be. The trick is to give it time. Just as no one walks into a gym and expects to build world-class muscles during the first session, your brain needs time to gain willpower. So, give "reflective consumption" time, and whenever you use it, think of it as a workout session that builds muscle slowly but surely. Over time, your self-discipline will grow, and before you know it, making wise financial decisions becomes second nature, almost effortless. You'll automatically evaluate each purchase, aligning spending with your long-term goals.

Moreover, this practice can significantly enhance emotional well-being. When deliberate and meaningful purchases contribute to a sense of purpose and satisfaction that spontaneous buying often fails to deliver. Over time, this leads to what psychologists call "congruence"—a harmony between your actions and your values, which you need for long-term happiness and fulfillment.

Back to your story: Determined, you decided to start small. You kept a notebook for a month, jotting down every purchase, no matter how tiny. It was eye-opening—you hadn't realized how much you spent on fast food and impulse buys (see exercise below). But the most significant part was asking yourself if the purchases held the potential to improve your life.

As you questioned whether each expense brought joy or only momentary satisfaction, a lightbulb went off, and you realized how short-lived the thrill of spending can be.

Oddly, this realization resonated with you—something you'd never expect—and it made you feel warm inside—a calming glow reminding you how fabulous it feels to be at peace. And while peace doesn't seem as much fun as indulging in one of those now-instead-of-later things, the truth is that **peace of mind feels better than anything**.

It surprised you when you realized there's something undeniably delightful about your newfound control. Whenever you skipped an impulse purchase, you saw each dollar join with the next, slowly building a tower of freedom. And at the top of the tower is your purpose—being free of debt and able to afford the things you *really* want to buy—a new home, for example. Encouraged by these insights, you expanded your efforts. You set a goal to reduce dining out and cook more meals at home. Each dish saved money, and you welcomed the challenge of improving your culinary skills. Watching your savings grow was far more rewarding than you had imagined.

The real test came when you won $1,000 at a charity event. Instead of splurging on the latest tech gadget, you paused, considering your new financial goals. You asked yourself if the purchase aligned with your priorities. It didn't. So, you redirected that money into your savings account, earmarking it for a life-changing purchase—a reward for your financial discipline.

As the months went by, you found new ways to smarten up your spending during budget check-ins. You opted for free services over subscriptions, walked instead of grabbing rides, and hit the community park programs for entertainment. Each choice boosted your savings, each trade-off fueled by your end goal.

Finally, the day came when you bought a house. The joy was profound, lasting, and deeper than any impulse purchase.

When you turned the key, you thought, *Wow. It's true. Controlling my destiny is my superpower!*

From then on, budgeting became an adventure—a tool to make dreams come true.

Here is another client success story. After struggling to stick to a budget on her own, she reached out for help. Together, we crafted a realistic budget, created a plan to pay down debt, and set up a savings strategy.

About six months later, her car broke down. In the past, this would have caused a lot of stress, but my client had been diligent in following the plan and had savings set aside. When she realized the repair costs were more than the car was worth, she confidently started looking for another vehicle, knowing she had enough money saved for a down payment and could still manage her bills. My client felt empowered because she knew she had money to put down for a car and still pay their bills. Anyone can achieve this success if you put in the work.

And yes, it's time for another exercise. This one will follow you over the next 30 days and help you conquer mindless spending. You'll love the **NEW YOU** at the end, so let's go!

Your 30-Day Reflection Adventure

Welcome to your 30-Day Reflection Adventure, where you'll develop mindful spending habits and improve your decision-making skills. This journaling exercise will guide you through reflecting on your spending, understanding your motivations, and aligning your purchases with your long-term financial goals.

Setting Up Your Reflection Adventure Journal

The following pages will be your companion throughout the next 30 days, helping you track your thoughts, desires, and decisions about spending. Make sure it's a place where you feel comfortable expressing your thoughts freely. Your 30 days begins the next time you want to buy a non-essential item—anything from a new outfit to theater tickets to a box of chocolates—something you'd love to have but it's not an emergency or a must.

Whenever you feel tempted to make a non-essential purchase, pause for a moment. Before you proceed, write down the item you're considering buying and its cost in your journal. Take some time to reflect on why you want this item.

Ask yourself how this purchase would improve your life. Be specific about the benefits you expect to gain. Will it bring you lasting happiness, or is it a momentary desire? Writing down these thoughts helps you connect with the real reasons behind your spending urges.

Over the next 30 days, revisit your journal entry daily and think about how you feel. Use the following daily prompts to guide you:

Day 1: How do I feel today? Is the desire to buy the item as strong as when I first thought about it?

Day 2: Have I thought about the item frequently today? If so, what triggered those thoughts?

Day 3: Does the item still feel necessary, or do I see it as a luxury?

Day 4: How would buying this item align with my financial goals and values?

Day 5: Reflecting on the past few days, is my desire for this purchase increasing, decreasing, or staying the same?

Day 6: If I had this item right now, how would it impact my life today?

Day 7: After a week of reflection, do I still feel excited about the potential purchase?

Day 8: What emotions am I experiencing when I think about buying this item?

Day 9: Have I noticed any alternative ways to fulfill the need or desire that this item represents?

Day 10: Would this purchase bring lasting value, or is it a temporary fix for something deeper?

Day 11: How does my current financial situation influence my thoughts about this purchase?

Day 12: Am I thinking about this item more or less than when I first wanted it?

Day 13: How would I feel if I decided not to buy this item at all?

Day 14: After two weeks, does the item still seem as important as it did initially?

Day 15: What benefits do I think this purchase will bring me, and are those benefits still appealing?

Day 16: Have I discussed this purchase with anyone? If so, how did that conversation influence my thoughts?

Day 17: Is there a better way to use the money I would spend on this item?

Day 18: How does delaying this purchase make me feel? Am I impatient or comfortable with waiting?

Day 19: Has the importance of this item in my life increased or decreased over the past 19 days?

Day 20: Am I still thinking about the item frequently, or has my interest waned?

Day 21: How do I think I'll feel if I buy this item now? Will the satisfaction last?

Day 22: If I had to decide today, would I buy this item or not?

Day 23: How would this purchase affect my other financial priorities?

Day 24: What would happen if I decided not to buy this item at all?

Day 25: Reflecting on the past few weeks, has my perception of this item changed?

Day 26: Would buying this item make me happier or just temporarily satisfied?

Day 27: How do I feel about the money I would spend on this item? Could it be better used elsewhere?

Day 28: As I near the end of this reflection, does this item still hold the same appeal?

Day 29: How has this 30-day reflection process affected my overall spending habits and thoughts?

Day 30: Now that 30 days have passed, do I still want to make this purchase? Why or why not?

Evaluate and Decide

At the end of the 30 days, review your daily reflections and evaluate your notes. Based on your reflection, make an informed decision about whether to proceed with the purchase or skip it. This step is crucial in developing the habit of mindful spending, and it lets you learn how important the purchase is to you. Have you ever planted a garden and watched it grow? When you first plant the seeds, there's a lot of anticipation and excitement. But you don't see immediate results—you have to wait, water, and nurture the plants over time. Each day, you might check in, wondering if today will be the day you see a sprout.

Spending can be similar. The idea of making a purchase is exciting, like planting a seed. But instead of rushing to buy, the 30-day exercise is like giving that seed time to grow. You're allowing your desire to either take root and grow stronger or fade away if it's not truly important.

At the end of the 30 days, you evaluate whether this "seed" has grown into something worth nurturing—a purchase that will bring lasting value—or if it's something that doesn't need to take up space in your life. By waiting and reflecting, you make sure that what you choose to "plant" in your financial garden is something that will truly blossom and bring you joy over time.

Reflect on the Process

Regardless of whether you choose to buy the item or not, take some time to reflect on what you learned about your spending habits and impulses. Write down any patterns or insights you noticed about your consumption behavior.

Did you find that certain triggers, emotions, or situations made you more likely to want to buy something? Did waiting 30 days help you see the purchase differently? Understanding these patterns is key to making more thoughtful decisions in the future.

The Benefits of Reflective Consumption

As you go through this 30-day exercise, you'll likely notice a shift in how you perceive value and make spending choices. Reflective consumption encourages you to pause and think deeply about your spending, linking it to your long-term goals and true needs.

Your 30-Day Reflection Adventure is a powerful tool for transforming your relationship with money. By practicing patience and mindfulness in your spending decisions, you're taking control of your financial future. Continue to use this journal beyond the 30 days and watch how your financial habits evolve and improve over time.

Remember, each step you take in this process brings you closer to financial freedom and peace of mind. Enjoy the journey and celebrate the progress you make along the way.

I Support You. I Believe in You.

Before we turn to the last chapter, I want to pause and share something personal. I've stood exactly where you are today. I remember the initial resistance—the cringe at the thought of journaling and especially undertaking the Reflection Adventure Exercise.

I, too, have wrestled with the thought, "I don't need this. I can control my spending alone; I don't have time for this nonsense."

It's natural to feel resistant. Confronting spending habits and questioning impulses can be uncomfortable. During the exercise, your vulnerabilities are brought to light, prompting you to confront habits that are easier to overlook.

Know this: **Your resistance signals the need for this exercise**. Reflective consumption goes beyond learning how to control your spending. What you want is to understand why you do what you do.

If someone offered you a million dollars to do the Reflection Adventure Exercise for one month, would you do it? Of course, you would. You'd start immediately! It's a no-brainer, right?

So, if the assurance of receiving a million dollars transforms the Reflection Adventure Exercise from a chore into an adventure, then it's not that you don't want to do the exercise; it's that there is nothing to excite you enough to do it.

The solution is to identify what excites you about financial freedom. Pinpoint your dreams that require financial backing—traveling the world, buying a home, or having a comfortable retirement. Turn your financial dreams into a thrill that propels you forward, and know that with the right commitment and mindset, a million dollars truly is on the line. How cool would it be if you started the Reflection Exercise a month ago? How far would you have come? So, start now knowing that, one month from now, while you might not have a million dollars *yet*, you'll feel like a million bucks.

Over time, your awareness will transform your budget, overall decision-making approach, and life priorities. **Your greatest insights come from stepping outside your comfort zone and challenging your assumptions.**

Alone or with Help? It's Up to You.

The next chapter is all about comforting and supporting yourself. While you have everything you need to succeed, I am here for you if you need me. Let's explore which path you'll take.

CHAPTER SIX

I Have Your Back

As you read this final chapter, I hope you'll take a moment to recognize your progress. Even if you've only lightly read this book once and have yet to do the exercises, your subconscious mind has absorbed everything and will continue working on what you've learned.

Let's recap the 5 Steps to Transform Your Relationship With Money:

1. **Understand your money story**

Take time to reflect on your financial beliefs and habits, especially those formed in childhood. Recognize any limiting beliefs or negative associations you have with money. Understanding the "why" behind your current behaviors can give you the clarity to start making positive changes.

2. **Shift your money mindset**

Develop a mindset focused on growth, abundance, and empowerment. Replace thoughts of scarcity with beliefs that support financial confidence and success. Practicing gratitude for what you have and visualizing your financial goals can help you create a positive and proactive attitude toward money.

3. **Set clear financial goals aligned with your values**

Define financial goals that align with your personal values and long-term aspirations. Whether it's saving for a home, becoming debt-free, or building generational wealth, having clear goals will help you stay motivated and focused.

4. **Build healthy financial habits**

Start implementing practical financial habits, like budgeting, saving consistently, and managing debt. Automate where possible, such as direct savings deposits, to make these habits effortless. Over time, these habits will replace any impulsive or reactive behaviors and become the foundation of your financial wellness.

5. **Track progress and celebrate milestones**

Regularly review your progress to stay accountable and adjust your plan if needed. Celebrate small victories along the way, whether it's paying down a portion of debt or reaching a savings milestone. Recognizing your achievements keeps you motivated and reinforces your commitment to a healthier financial future.

Before you know it, you will find the motivation to put everything in place.

Have you heard this old joke? It's a classic: **A tourist in New York City asks a local, "How do you get to Carnegie Hall?"**
The local replies, "Practice."

Now that you have the knowledge and tools needed, remember this is only the beginning. As with any worthwhile endeavor, managing money takes practice if you want to master your financial well-being.

This is Only the Beginning

I invite you to join my community through a free monthly newsletter through my website at https://www.sensiblelivingcoach.com/. You'll get inspiration, reminders, and practical tips to maintain your financial well-being. Think of them as your monthly financial fitness check-in, helping you stay on track and grow in your financial life.

Our community encourages and motivates you to pursue your financial goals. Each newsletter gives you success stories, actionable advice, and the latest insights in personal finance. Consider it your monthly dose of inspiration, helping you stay motivated and informed.

While newsletters and community support are invaluable, sometimes you need a more personalized approach. Have you noticed you perform better with accountability?

Imagine you've decided to run a marathon. It's a big goal, and while crossing that finish line is exhilarating, the journey can be overwhelming. But then, you find a running buddy—a friend who also dreams of completing a marathon. Suddenly, your solo runs become a social event filled with encouragement, shared progress, and laughs. Ah, the magic of accountability!

That's where Sensible Living Coach comes in. You'll succeed faster, turning a tedious task into a fun and engaging adventure. And if you hit a financial snag or face unexpected challenges, instead of feeling stressed or overwhelmed, you'll have a trusted partner to offer solutions and support.

As an advanced expert in financial wellness, I offer private consultations to give you tailored advice and strategies—everything from refining budgeting skills to overcoming challenges. I can even be your exercise buddy as we walk through every exercise together (which, by the way, is a blast!)

I have your back, and I welcome hearing from you. Go to https://www.sensiblelivingcoach.com/ to schedule a complementary 15-minute consultation. Or message me on Instagram @sensiblelivingcoach to let me know if this book was beneficial. **Are You Ready?**

"Even the greatest was once a beginner. Don't be afraid to take that first step." — Muhammad Ali

No matter how small, every step you take, whether saving a bit each month or investing wisely, contributes to building a more secure and prosperous financial future. Challenges teach valuable lessons, foster personal growth, and strengthen resilience, shaping you into a more financially savvy individual prepared for whatever the future holds.

Close this book, take a deep breath, and celebrate your progress (keep it within budget, of course!)

Always move forward with confidence and determination. You are about to become stronger, wiser, and empowered.

Happiness is your new best friend.